CORAL REEFS
COLORFUL UNDERWATER HABITATS

PICTURE WINDOW BOOKS
Minneapolis, Minnesota

BY LAURA PURDIE SALAS   ILLUSTRATED BY JEFF YESH

Thanks to our advisers for their expertise, research, and advice:

Cynthia Hunter, Ph.D., Associate Professor of Marine Biology
University of Hawaii, Honolulu

Terry Flaherty, Ph.D., Professor of English
Minnesota State University, Mankato

Editor: Shelly Lyons
Designer: Lori Bye
Page Production: Melissa Kes
Art Director: Nathan Gassman
Editorial Director: Nick Healy

The illustrations in this book were created digitally.

Picture Window Books
151 Good Counsel Drive
P.O. Box 669
Mankato, MN 56002-0669
877-845-8392
www.picturewindowbooks.com

Photo Credits: DigitalVision, 23

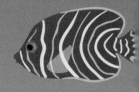

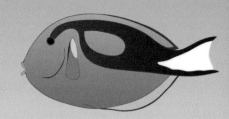

 All books published by Picture Window Books
are manufactured with paper containing at least
10 percent post-consumer waste.

Library of Congress Cataloging-in-Publication Data
Salas, Laura Purdie.
Coral reefs : colorful underwater habitats / by Laura Purdie Salas ;
illustrated by Jeff Yesh.
p. cm. — (Amazing Science: Ecosystems)
ISBN 978-1-4048-5373-7 (library binding)
1. Coral reef ecology—Juvenile literature. 2. Coral reefs and
islands—Juvenile literature. I. Yesh, Jeff, 1971- ill. II. Title.
QH541.5.C7S25 2009
577.7'89—dc22   2008037899

Table of Contents

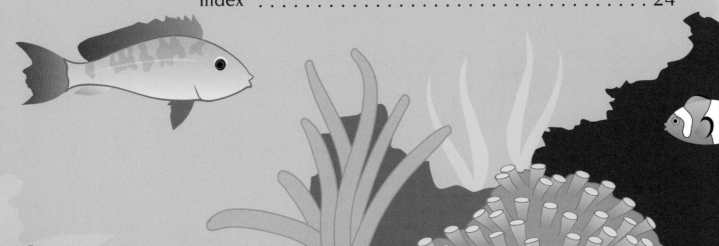

Living and Colorful

Sunlight sparkles in the ocean water that surrounds you. A bright, living garden lies on the ocean floor beneath you. Millions of sea creatures live in this underwater community. A blue tang fish swims among branching corals, some hard and some soft. Crabs, snails, worms, and many other creatures hide in holes.

Welcome to the colorful coral reef ecosystem. An ecosystem is all of the living and nonliving things in a certain area. It includes plants, animals, water, soil, weather ... everything!

Fun Fact

Some people call the coral reef the rain forest of the ocean. On land, rain forests contain lots of animals and plants. Coral reefs also have many different kinds of underwater life.

Where Are Coral Reefs?

Coral reef communities depend on warm temperatures. Because of this, coral reefs are found near Earth's equator. They form in warm, clear, shallow water.

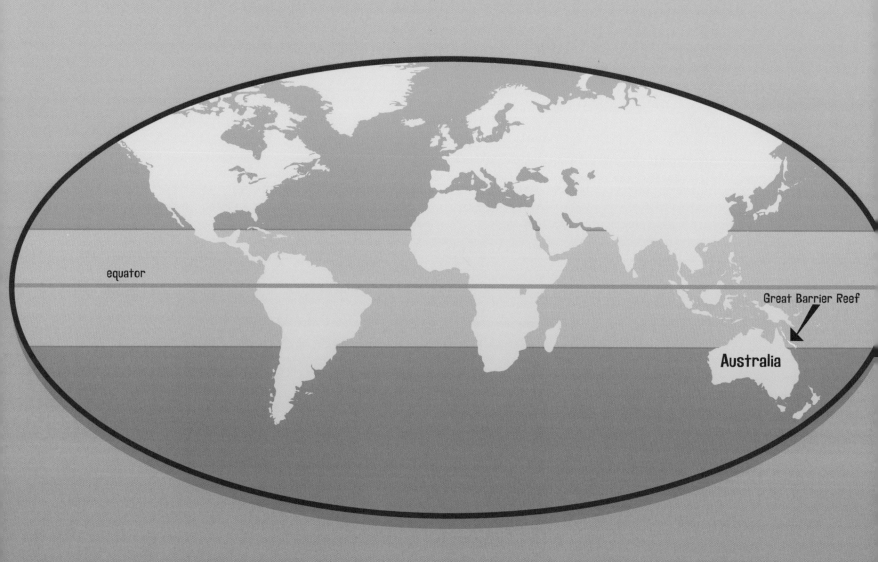

equator

Great Barrier Reef

Australia

Fun Fact

All of Earth's coral reefs are in an area just north or south of the equator. Most coral reefs do not show up on pictures taken from outer space. However, Australia's Great Barrier Reef is so large, it is visible from outer space!

Coral reefs are located in three underwater areas. Most reefs are called fringing reefs. They lie close to land. Barrier reefs form farther out. They are separated from land by a lagoon, or shallow body of water. Atolls are tiny reefs that become islands on top of inactive underwater volcanoes.

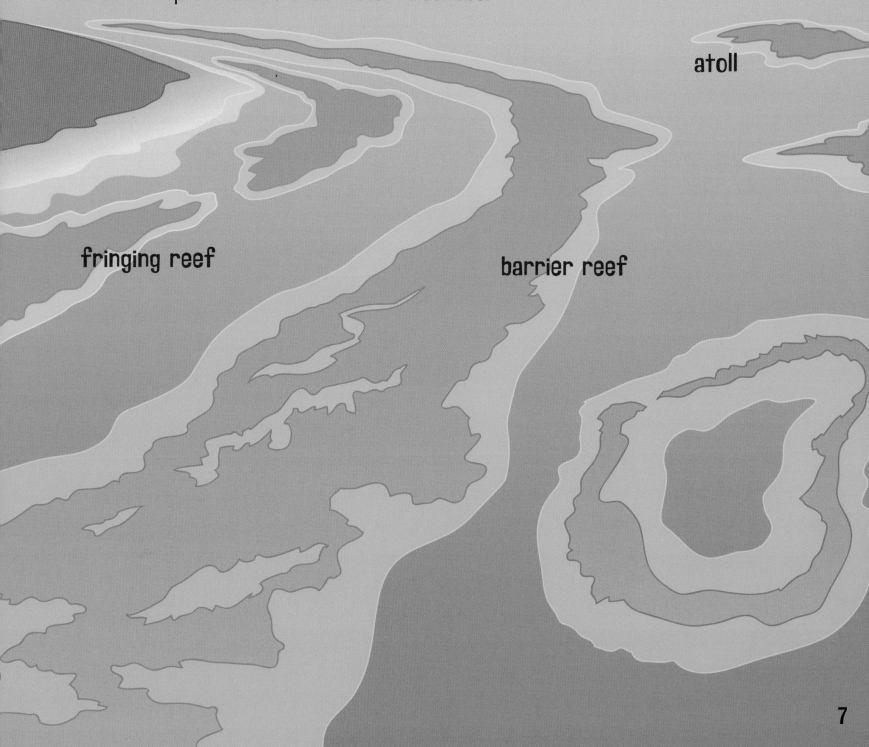

atoll

fringing reef

barrier reef

How Coral Reefs Form

Corals may look like plants or rocks. Reef corals are actually the skeletons of soft animals called polyps. Polyps live in one spot all of their adult lives. They make skeletons to protect themselves.

Most often, polyps live in huge groups called colonies. As they die, other polyps build right on top of the empty skeletons. The skeletons pile up to form a reef. It can take hundreds or even thousands of years for the skeletons to form a reef.

Fun Fact

Only the outer layer of corals in a coral reef contains living polyps. Think of the coral reef as a city full of skyscrapers. The buildings are all empty, except for their top floors.

polyps

Animals of the Coral Reef

So many animals live in the coral reef! Thousands of different kinds of fish live there, such as spiny leaf fish and parrot fish. So do crabs, sea stars, sea turtles, and octopuses. Sharks and other large animals visit the reef, hunting for smaller animals. These animals feed, hide, and give birth. They swim, dart, and drift throughout the reef.

parrot fish

shark

Fun Fact
A parrot fish has teeth like a beak. With its beak, the fish grinds up the reef as it eats algae. The ground-up corals later wash ashore and become part of sandy beaches.

sea turtle

spiny leaf fish

sea star

Algae: Base of the Food Chain

Plants, especially tiny algae, are important to coral reef ecosystems. Algae live inside of the cells of coral polyps. Coral polyps share nutrients with the algae. The algae also have a protected place to live inside of the polyps.

algae

What do the polyps get? Like all plants, when algae receive sunlight, they make food and a gas called oxygen. Polyps get food and oxygen in return for the nutrients and protection they give the algae.

Fun Fact

Corals can be pink, blue, brown, green, orange, yellow, and purple. The algae also add some color. They are orange or brown. If the water gets too warm, corals might let out the algae. If the corals turn white when the algae are gone, it is called coral bleaching.

Other Coral Reef Plants

Algae are not the only plants found in coral reefs. Most scientists consider mangroves and sea grasses part of this ecosystem, too.

Mangroves are trees and shrubs that grow above ground, near shore. They can survive in salt water and often grow near coral reefs.

Fun Fact

Mangrove roots trap mud and small pieces of things that wash away from the land. The roots help keep the water clear. Because the water is clear, more sunlight reaches the coral reef and the algae. In this way, mangroves help keep the coral polyps alive.

Sea grasses are flowering plants that grow underwater but need sunlight.
Animals such as sea horses and anemones live among the sea grass meadows.
Many reef animals, like sea turtles, eat sea grasses.

sea horse

anemone

Coral Reefs in Action

Coral reefs do many things. Reefs give young fish and small sea animals a safe place to grow up. Lots of hiding places help keep sea animals safe.

Coral reefs also protect Earth's coastlines. Ocean waves slam into the reefs and grow weaker before reaching shore. Coral reefs keep our coastlines from eroding, or wearing away.

People also want to see the beauty of coral reefs. Many people depend on the money that tourists bring when they visit coral reef areas. People also depend on the food that coral reefs provide.

Destruction and Regrowth

Weather is the biggest natural threat to the coral reef. Coral reefs form in shallow water, where pounding waves can break the corals. Reefs can grow back. Some corals grow as little as 0.1 inch (0.25 centimeter) in a year. Those corals would take more than two years to grow as long as your pencil eraser! Other corals grow as much as 4 inches (10.2 cm) in a year. With much time, coral reefs can regrow after storms.

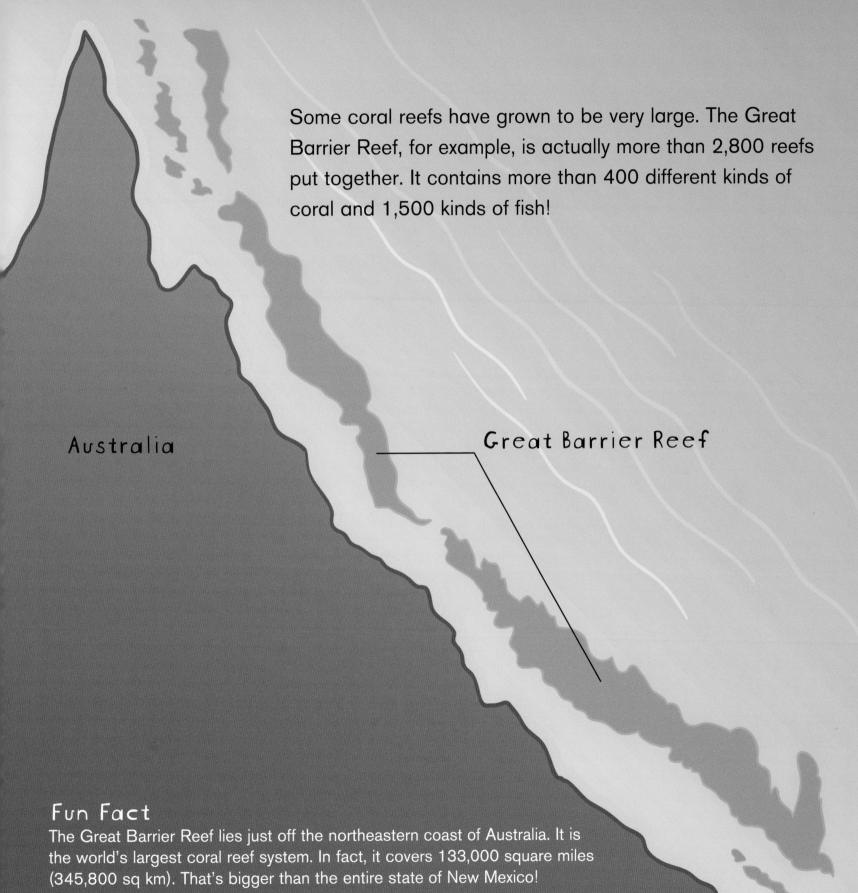

Some coral reefs have grown to be very large. The Great Barrier Reef, for example, is actually more than 2,800 reefs put together. It contains more than 400 different kinds of coral and 1,500 kinds of fish!

Australia

Great Barrier Reef

Fun Fact

The Great Barrier Reef lies just off the northeastern coast of Australia. It is the world's largest coral reef system. In fact, it covers 133,000 square miles (345,800 sq km). That's bigger than the entire state of New Mexico!

Coral Reefs in Danger

People are a much bigger threat to coral reefs. The pollution we create, especially waste from factories and large farms, is a big problem. Pollution makes the ocean water cloudy and keeps sunlight from reaching polyps and algae.

Fishing boats sometimes scrape against coral reefs, cracking apart the corals. Divers sometimes break off pieces of coral to sell.

Fun Fact
Overfishing also harms reefs. If people catch too many fish, there aren't enough fish left to eat the algae. If there's too much algae, it will kill off the corals.

Coral reefs are an important ecosystem in our world. They are home to many fish and animals that we depend on for food. They also protect our shores. For these reasons, we should learn to enjoy beautiful coral reefs without harming them.

Coral Reef Diorama: Coral Reef in a Box

What You Need:

- a shoebox
- colorful acrylic paints
- construction paper
- self-drying modeling clay
- assorted rocks (clean and dry)

- glue
- foam tape
- pipe cleaners
- pictures of coral reef animals, such as fish, turtles, and crabs

What You Do:

1. Turn the shoebox on its side.

2. Paint the bottom blue, and paint the sides and top a lighter blue.

3. Paint rocks the colors of corals. Use glue or foam tape to arrange them across the bottom.

4. Make branching corals from pipe cleaners. Arrange them in the cracks between rocks.

5. Use colored paper, clay, or pictures to make the animals of the coral reef. Make your reef lively and colorful!

Coral Reef Facts

- Corals come in all shapes and colors. There are corals that look like daisies, cactuses, brains, fans, and antlers.

- The Great Barrier Reef is the biggest structure on Earth made by living creatures.

- Hurricanes and other natural causes may harm coral reefs. But the actions of humans can cause much more harm to coral reefs.

Coral reef

Glossary

algae—plants that live in water; some are huge and some are very tiny

atoll—a tiny reef that becomes an island on top of an underwater volcano

barrier reef—a reef that forms farther offshore than a fringing reef

cells—basic parts of animals or plants that are so small you can't see them without a microscope

community—a group of living organisms that live in one area

ecosystem—an area with certain animals, plants, weather, and land or water features

equator—an imaginary line around the middle of Earth; it divides the northern half from the southern half

fringing reef—a reef that forms close to land and grows outward from the shoreline

lagoon—shallow area of water between the coast and a coral reef that's offshore

nutrients—parts of food, like vitamins, that are used for growth

oxygen—a gas that people and animals must breathe to stay alive

To Learn More

More Books to Read

Berkes, Marianne Collins. *Over in the Ocean in a Coral Reef.* Nevada City, Calif.: Dawn Publications, 2004.

Galko, Francine. *Coral Reef Animals.* Chicago: Heinemann Library, 2003.

Gibbons, Gail. *Coral Reefs.* New York: Holiday House, 2007.

Gray, Susan Heinrichs. *Coral Reefs.* Minneapolis: Compass Point Books, 2001.

On the Web

FactHound offers a safe, fun way to find educator-approved Internet sites related to this book.

Here's what you do:
1. Visit *www.facthound.com*
2. Choose your grade level.
3. Begin your search.

This book's ID number is 9781404853737

Index

Look for all of the books in the Amazing Science—Ecosystems series:

Coral Reefs: Colorful Underwater Habitats
Deserts: Thirsty Wonderlands
Grasslands: Fields of Green and Gold
Oceans: Underwater Worlds
Rain Forests: Gardens of Green
Temperate Deciduous Forests: Lands of Falling Leaves
Tundras: Frosty, Treeless Lands
Wetlands: Soggy Habitat

DATE DUE

SE 0 2 '10 SE 2 3 '10			
NO 1 8 '10			
DE 0 6 '10			
AG 2 7 '12			
JY 0 3 '13			
GAYLORD			PRINTED IN U.S.A.